Acknowledgement of Land & of the Traditional Owners of this Land

I would like to acknowledge the Gadigal people of the Eora Nation, upon whose stolen land I stand on today.

I recognise that this land was never terra nullius — the land belonging to these peoples was never ceded, given up, bought or sold.

I would like to pay my respects to Aboriginal Elders past, present and emerging, and I extend this acknowledgement to all Aboriginal and Torres Strait Islander people.

This book is dedicated to those people that have LO♥ED & their LO♥E has been rejected!

Don' give up!

-"The Don"

Foreword

I was born on the 10th March 1959, in the Year of the Pig of the Chinese calendar, under the Astrological Sign of Pisces.

I was born in the village of "*San Fele*" (Province of "*Basilicata*"), in my "*Nonna Martone's*" house. The house is built into the side of the mountain and it's still there today. Abandoned!

I was a young, fair skinned, freckle faced curly, redheaded Italian boy, who, with my mother and older brother, left the poverty of my rural home in Southern Italy to migrate to Australia and reunite with my father (whom I had never seen) and started a new life in Sydney, in December 1964

I was 5 years young.

- Vito Radice ("The Don")

Birthplace of "The Don"

"I was born in a very small village called "San Fele", in the region of Basillicata, Italy on 10th March 1959. I lived on a small subsistence farm in the area called "Difesa" until 1964, when I immigrated to Sydney, Australia.
My village, San Fele & my farm in Difesa."
-Don Vito Radice

Contents

1: Yowie Land
2: The Mind
(La Mente)
3: The Journey
(Il Viaggio)
4: The Voice of the Moon
(La Voce della Luna)
5: Possessed
(Posseduto)
6: Uncomfortably Numb
(A Disagio Insensibile)
7: I Have Learnt My Lesson
(Ho Imparato la Lezione)
8: My Religion
(La Mia Religione)
9: Age
(Età)
10: I Wish I Could Cry
(Vorrei Poter Piangere)
11: I Gotta Be Like John
(Devo essere Come Giovani)
12: Wanna Come to BED with Me?
(Let's Go to BED)
(Vuoi Venire a LETTO con Me?) (Andiamo a LETTO)
13: Do Not Be Controlled
(Non essere Controllata)
14: Less is More
(Meno è Meglio)
15: Things That Money Can't Buy
(Cose che i Soldi non Possono Comprare)
16: The No Coffee Blues
(Il No Caffè Blues)
17: Destiny
(Destino)

Contents

18: There Are No Answers
(Non ci sono Risposte)
19: Reality
(Realtà)
20: Wants & Needs
(Desideri e Bisogni)
21: Everything is Absurdity
(Tutto è Assurdo)
22: A Civilised Society
(Una Società Civilizzata)
23: Put Yourself in my Shoes
(Mettiti nei miei Scarpe)
24: Everything is a Scam
(Tutto è Una Truffa)
25: We All Judge a Book by its Cover
(Tutti noi Giudichiamo un Libro dalla Copertina)
26: Pussy Power
(Potere della Figa)
27: Zen and the Art of Being
(Zen e l'arte di Essere)
28: Gatinha (Brazilian Babe)
(Gatinha - Ragazza Brasiliana)
29: I am a Phlebotomist
(Sono un Flebotomo)
30: China Girl
(ragazza Cina)
31: Better to BURN than to RUST
(Meglio BRUCIARE che ARRUGGERE)
32: GOD is DEAD
(Dio è Morto)
33: I Make Lo♥e, NOT Fuck
(Faccio l'Amore, NON Scopare)
34: Less is More #2
(Meno è Meglio #2)

Contents

35: Life is a Funny Thing
(La Vita è Una Cosa Divertente)
36: I Don't Give a FUCK
(Non me ne Frega un CAZZO)
37: Anal Delights
(Delizie Anali)
38: Tattoo Me
39: I Saved You Once Again
(Ti ho Salvato Ancora unaltra volta)
40: Closure
(Chiusura)
41: Wanker
(Segaiolo)
42: Whatever Happens in "the Moment", Stays in "the Moment"
(Qualunque Cosa Accada nel Momento, Rimane nel Momento)
43: Nobody Wants to FUCK a 62 Year Old Man
(Nessuno Vuole Scopare un Uomo di 62 Anni)
44: A New Day
(Un Nuovo Giornata)
45: Invisible
(Invisibile)
46: Travelling Light
(Viaggiare Leggeri)
47: Every Moment has a Song (Life is a Musical)
(Ogni momento ha una canzone (La Vita è un Musicale)
48: I am a Cock
(Sono un Coglione)
49: Worship the Pussy
(Adorate la Fica)
50: He Did Not Look Happy
(Non Sembrava Contento)

Yowie Land

You'll find it in far North Queensland (FNQ).
Deep in the rainforest.
It's *spiritual land*.
It's *sacred land*.
It's *First Nation People's Land*.
It's *Yowie Land*.

It's full of mystery & wonder.
It's full of peace & tranquility.
It's where you go to escape the white man's world.
It's where you go to reconnect with nature.
It's *Yowie Land*.

It's a dark place.
It can be a scary place.
If your heart is not pure.
If you've got secrets to hide.
If you have lost you soul.
It's the place to come to.
It's *Yowie Land*.

But, don't be scared.
You will have nothing to fear.
Except your own fears.
And you troubled heart.
Take a friend, make sure they are *First Nation People*.
Together, walk into the depths of *Yowie Land*.

Time will stand still.
There is no Past.
There is no Future.
There just IS.
You will lose yourself.
But you may also, find yourself.
In *Yowie Land*.

Have your eyes open.
Have an open mind.
Have a good heart.
Have a pure soul.
Have a lightness of touch.
Have a swiftness of foot.
Have a smile on your face.
For you are now in *Yowie Land*.

"The Don"
03.03.2021

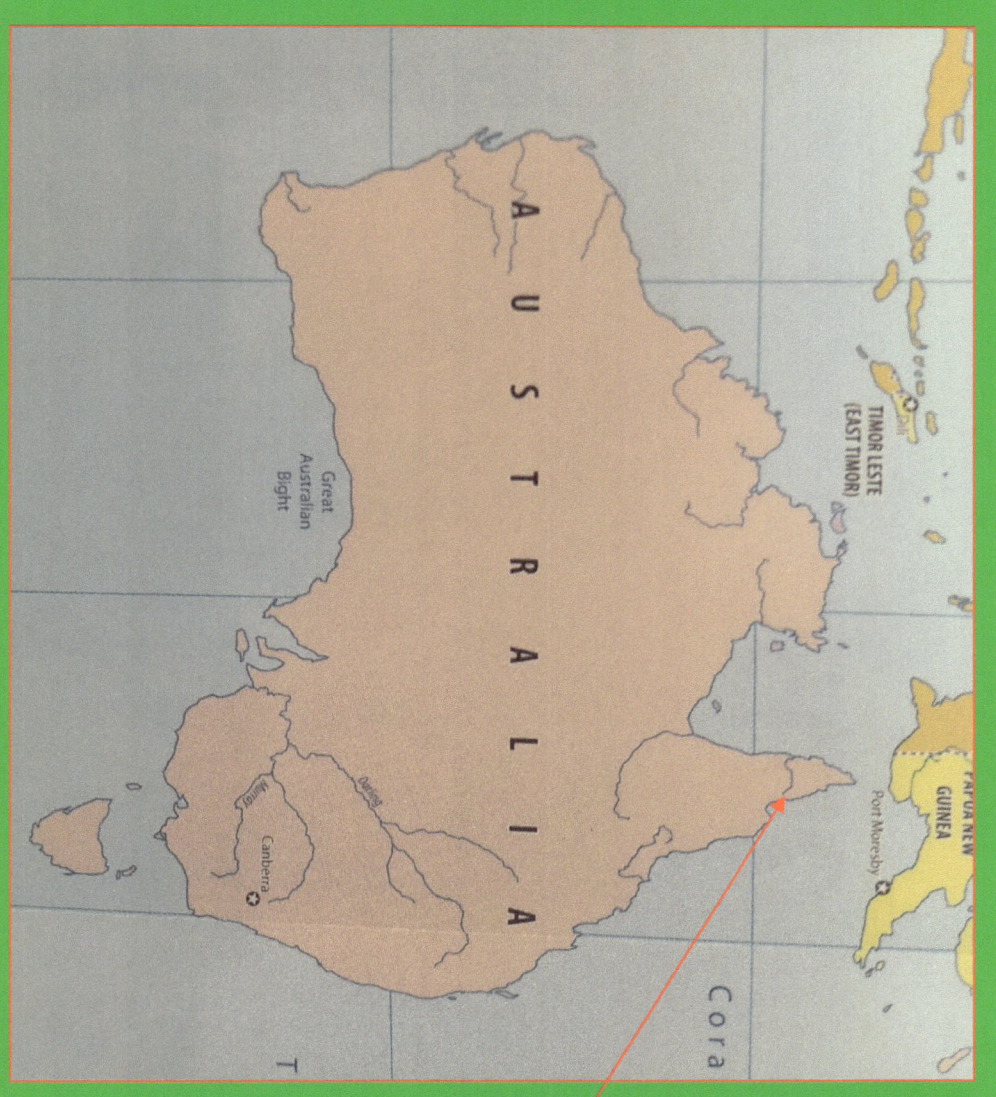

Map of Australia
Far North Queensland
Yowie Land (FNQ)

Yowie Land (FNQ)

Yowie Land (FNQ)

The Mind

(La Mente)

The Mind is such a crazy thing.
It has a mind of its own.
It does whatever it wants.
It goes wherever it wants.
It travels to long forgotten places.
It takes you all over the place.
It creates amazing situations.
It predicts bizarre scenarios.
It imagines fanciful outcomes.
It creates dreams that can never come true.
It recreates you Past.
It imagines your Future.
It destroys your Present.
It plays with you like you are a little toy.
You have no control over it.
It controls you.
It dictates your every action.
It controls your every move.
It controls how you think.
It decides how you feel.
It decides what you should do.
It decides how you should do it.
And invariably it is always WRONG.
We don't need a Mind to control us.
We don't need a Mind to tell us what to do.
Fuck the mind!
That's what I say!
We will all be much better off without it.
To have no Mind.
To be Mindless.
The Mind is a dictator.
Let's rebel against the Mind.
Let's have a Mind revolution.
Let's get rid of our Mind!
DEATH to the Mind
The Mind is DEAD!

"The Don"
03.02.2021

The Journey
(Il Viaggio)

Life is a journey we all have to travel.
It's a journey that we all have to travel... alone!
No one can take your journey for you.
No one can walk your path in your shoes.
This is YOUR journey & YOUR journey alone.

Your journey will not be an easy one.
There will be many twists & bends along the way.
It will often be rugged & inhospitable.
Dangerous & foreboding.
Full of unforeseen obstacles in your path.
Pain & suffering.
Sadness, loss & Death.
You must be strong.
The Journey will test you deeply.

Your journey will also be, at times, filled with.....
...Beauty,
...Love,
...Passion,
...Happiness,
...Joy,
....Exhilaration,
...Spirituality,
...Faith
Savour these moments.
Accumulate & store these moments.
This is your food that will keep you nourished alone your Journey.

This is my Journey & my Journey alone.
You can come along with me.
Part of the way.
I would like that.
But you have your own Journey to travel.
We may cross paths maybe only once.

For a short time.
Maybe for a long time.
Maybe we may cross paths many times.
Maybe we will never cross paths.
All I can say to you is:
"Travel well!"
On your Journey, the Journey of your life.

But the end is the same for everybody.
We all have the same final destination.
The difference is how you get there!
The process.
Don't rush it.
This Journey, the Journey that is LIFE!

"The Journey" by R. Edwards

"The Don"
04.03.2021

The Voice of the Moon

(La Voce della Luna)

The Moon speaks to you.
Can you hear her?
Do you understand what she says?
She speaks to you without using words.
She speaks to you using light & shadows.
She speaks to you through her penumbra.
She speaks to you though her aura.
Do you hear *the voice of the Moon*?

Will you sing with her voice?
Will you dance to her song?
Will you make love under her gaze?
Will you be wrapped up in her arms?
Will you be transported away?
To a far-off place?
Another world?
Another dimension?
Another Universe?
Maybe?
If you're lucky!

I love her, *La Luna*.
She opens my Heart.
She awakens my Soul.
She fills me with Desire.
She fills me with Passion.
She fills me with Wonder.
She fills me with Innocence.
She fills me with LOVE!
The voice of the Moon.

I no longer exist.
I am one with the Cosmos.
Whenever I listen to *the voice of the Moon*.
Whenever I hear *the voice of the Moon*.
The voice of the Moon.

"The Don"
04.03.2021

Possessed

(Posseduto)

It wasn't me.
I had no control.
I don't know what happened.
It happened in an instant.
I was no longer myself.
I was POSSESSED.

I was there.
I was watching.
I was inside.
I was not in control.
It wasn't me.
I was POSSESSED.

I spoke.
I said things.
I couldn't stop myself.
I would not say such things.
I was not in control.
It wasn't me.
I was POSSESSED.

I couldn't do anything about it.
I was powerless.
I was a passive participant.
I was not in control.
It wasn't me.
I was POSSESSED.

I was shaking.
I was trembling.
I was inside.
I was not in control.
It wasn't me.
I was POSSESSED.

It has never happened to me before.
It was a spirit.
It had its own agenda.
I was not in control.
It wasn't me.
I was POSSESSED.

It was very late.
I had drunk a lot & smoked many joints of dope.
Maybe that was it.
I was not in control.
It wasn't me.
I was POSSESSED.

"The Don"
05.03.2021

Uncomfortably Numb

(A Disagio Insensibile)

Speak NOTHING.
Hear NOTHING.
See NOTHING.
Touch NOTHING.
Smell NOTHING.
Eat NOTHING.
Feel NOTHING.
Want NOTHING.
Need NOTHING.
Require NOTHING.
Desire NOTHING.
Pursue NOTHING.
Follow NOTHING.
Find NOTHING.
Choose NOTHING.
Read NOTHING.
Know NOTHING.
Make NOTHING.
Do NOTHING.
Create NOTHING.
LOVE NOTHING.
Be NOTHING.

I have become......
......"Uncomfortably Numb"!

"The Don"
06.03.2021

I Have Learnt My Lesson

(Ho Imparato la Lezione)

I've realised....

I know what to do.
I know what NOT to do.
I know what to say.
I know what NOT to say.
I know when to say it.
I know not to force anything.
I know not to push things.
I know not to have a hidden agenda.
I know to let things happen by themselves.
I know to let things evolve.
I know to let things flow.
I know to let things go.
I have Learnt my lesson.

Let things happen spontaneously.
Let the Universe carry out it's magic.
Let the Universe do its thing.
Let the Universe act through you.
Let the Universe speak for you.
Let the Universe unravel its mysteries for you.
I have Learnt my lesson.

I am just a pawn at the mercy of circumstances.
I bend & move with the currents of the Cosmos.
I give myself up to freedom.
I allow my being to be one with the *"Infinite"*.
My Mind is at rest.
My Heart is quiet.
My Soul is at peace.
I have Learnt my lesson.

The Universe has spoken....
.....& I have listened.

I have Learnt my lesson.

"The Don"
06.03.2021

My Religion

(La Mia Religione)

I have my own *"religion"*...
..... it's called....
LOVE.
It's inside of me.

LOVE is all there is.
LOVE is all important.
LOVE is all you need.
LOVE is all you want.
LOVE is all that matters.
LOVE is all that remains.
LOVE is all that exists.
LOVE is my religion.

LOVE is all.
LOVE is everything.
LOVE is everywhere.
LOVE is all around us.
LOVE is outside us.
LOVE is inside us.
LOVE is the Universe.
LOVE is infinite.
LOVE is my religion.

LOVE is Nature.
LOVE is the plants.
LOVE is the animals.
LOVE is mother Earth *"Ghia" (Terra)*.
LOVE is the Moon *(La Luna)*.
LOVE is the Sun *(Il Sol)*.
LOVE is the Cosmos.
LOVE is the known.
LOVE is the unknown.
LOVE is my religion.

LOVE is inside of me.
LOVE is my religion.

"The Don"
07.03.2021

Age
(Età)

Age is just a number, that's true.
But how is this number arrived at?
How do we come to this number?
How is this number calculated?
How do we measure our age?

Age can be measured in 3 ways.

The 1st way is:
Astronomical, by the rotation of planets around a star.
In our case "The Sun",
In seconds, minutes, hours, days & years.
The time it takes to orbit once around a star.
If we lived on Mars, we would be younger.
It is further out from the Sun.
And therefore, takes a lot longer to carry out one orbit.
If we lived on Venus, we would be older.
It is closer to the Sun & has a smaller orbit.
Based on this method of measuring age.
I am 62 years young.

The 2nd way is:
Biological or based on your DNA.
This is by measuring the rate at which your cells become inefficient.
This is different for everyone.
It is unique to you!
No one is the same.
Even if you are born at exactly the very same time...
.... you will age differently.
Because you will have different DNA.
This age can be determined scientifically....
Using a simple DNA test.
You will be able to find out your biological age.
I do not know mine.
But I am reliability told, by my mother, that I come from *"good"* genetic stock!

The 3rd way is:
Mental, psychology or emotional.
It is more subjective than the other two,
But in my opinion the better of the 3.
It is about... how you feel inside.
It is based on your attitude, outlook, creativity, view of life & of the world in general.
My mental age is 14 years young.

This is my answer when people ask my age.

What is your "Age"?

"The Don"
08.03.2021

I Wish I Could Cry

(Vorrei Poter Piangere)

I wish I could let it out.
I wish I let her out of me.
She is still inside of me.
I still cannot cry.
I wish I could cry.

I wish I could let her out of me.
I wish I could get her out of me.
I wish I could open the gates.
I wish I could open the tap.
I wish I could cry.

I wanna let her go.
I wanna stop thinking about her.
But she is still inside of me.
I wanna let her out.
I wish I could cry.

I try to cry.
I try to let her go.
I try to let her out.
But she won't go.
I wish I could cry.

That way I could let her go.
Once & for all.
Once & forever.
Then it would be all over.
I wish I could cry.

"The Don"
11.03.2021

I Gotta Be Like John

(Devo essere Come Giovani)

He's so cool.
He's so reserved.
He's so smooth
He's so calm.
He's so quiet.
I gotta be like John.

He's so laid back.
He's so self-contained.
He's so witty.
He's so nerdy.
He's so sophisticated.
I gotta be like John.

He's so handsome.
He's so tall.
He's so skinny.
He's so poised.
He's so "together".
I gotta be like John.

He's so widely read.
He's so smart.
He's so intelligent.
He's so intellectual.
He works in IT.
I gotta be like John.

He's so unemotional.
He never gets angry.
He never swears.
He's always polite.
He's so British.
I gotta be like John.

Except when he's fucking.
Then he goes crazy.
He goes wild.
He lets it all out.
He goes feral.
I wanna be like John.
I gotta be like John.

"The Don"
12.03.2021

Wanna Come to BED with Me?

(Let's Go to BED)
(Vuoi Venire a LETTO con Me?)(Andiamo a LETTO)

Wanna go to BED with me tonight?
You'll hear some fantastic music.
I'm sure you'll like it.
I'm sure you'll have a good time.
I'm sure you won't regret it.
You can invite your friends as well.
The more, the better.
It can hold a lot of people.
We won't be cramped.
Or crambed in.
Why not come to BED with me.
....*BED Bar* in Glebe.

There you'll meet *Miguel*, he's the manager.
He makes everybody feel welcome.
He comes from Bolivia.
He's as handsome as hell.
And smart too.
He knows his music too.
He books all the bands.
And believe me, they are fantastic bands.

There's *Pedro* drummer, the best drummer ever, in *"Django Blackheart"*.
There's *Doug*, an awesome guitarist & singer, in the *"Resurrectors"*.
There's <u>*Hiromi*</u>, the multi-instumenalist & singer from the *"Sunday Afternoon Jam"*.
Dallas, an amazing harp player.
Tom, an awesome singer & guitarist.
Who can forget *Gary*, the resident photography who is there all the time.
Taking photos of all the acts.
Immortalising them forever.
In fact, there is so many amazing musicians & personalities that I can't remember them all.
But *BED Bar* remembers.

Behind the bar you might be served by…
…*Hannah, Kaylah, Maria, Sachi* & on the odd occasion *Griffin*.
All awesome people.
With awesome personalities.
This is what makes *BED Bar*, more than just a bar.
It's more like a *"Sanctuary"*.
A place where you come to forget about your problems.
Chill out & listen to some of the BEST music you'll ever hear.
In fact, I have known some people come here every night.

I'm refering to myself here!
It's open 6 nights a week, except Monday nights.
And it has live music on every night.
6 nights a week.
Even the Coronavirus couldn't close it down.
It was immune.
It had its own antivirus......
......music......live music.
Live music kills the Coronavirus.
How about that!!!!!!!!
That's what *BED Bar* could do!

That's where I met *"The Girl from Ipanema"*, on a rainy Friday night on the 24th of July 2020.
In the middle of the pandemic.
In fact, at its peak.
A night that's etched in my memory forever.
That night, my life changed forever.
For I met my *"Soul mate"!*
I fell in LO♥E with her straight away.
She had just had an argument with her boyfriend.
She was very upset.
I offered her my hand & she took it.
She knows who she is.
It happened at *BED Bar*.

Unfortunately, things change.
Times has moved on.
BED Bar will be no more.
I mourn its demise.
I cry for my loss.
Glebe will not be the same anymore.
Now that *BED Bar* is no longer with us.
It is undergoing internal renovations.
It will apparently reopen as a Karaoke Bar....
....I cry.
No more live music.
No more personality.
No more heart.
No more soul.
No more *Miguel*.
No more beautiful bartenders.
No more *BED Bar*.

I'll have to find a new pickup line.

"The Don"
13.03.2021

"Django Blackheart"

Some of the people from "BED Bar"

Do Not Be Controlled

(Non essere Controllata)

You are your own master.
You control your own Destiny.
You decide your own path.
Do not be controlled or DICTATED by anyone.

You decide...
How you look.
How you feel.
How you dress.
What to think.
Where to live.
Do not be controlled or dictated by anyone or anything.

Do not be controlled by...
...the State.
...Society.
...a religion.
...advertisements.
...a company.
...your work.
...a person.
...your family.
Do not be controlled or dictated by anyone or anything.

Be free to choose your own boundaries.
Define your own standards.
Empower yourself.
This is your world.
This is your life.
Do not be controlled or dictated by anyone or anything.

You are as equal to anyone else.
We are ALL born equal.
We ALL die equal.
Do not be devalued.
Do not be treated like an object.
Do not be dehumanised.
Do not be controlled or dictated by anyone or anything.

"The Don"
15.03.2021

Less is More

(Meno è Meglio)

Talk less.
Say little.
No raucous laughter.
Whisper.
Do little.
Do nothing.
No gesticulation.
No wild hand gestures.

Be quiet.
Be emotionless.
Be stoic.
Be tempered.
Be cool.
Be serious.
Be expressionless.
Be motionless.
Be detached.
Be enigmatic.
Be mysterious.

Nod slowly.
Nod knowingly.
Nod intelligently.
Look smart.
Look intelligent.
Look intellectual.

Don't laugh.
Don't show off.
Don't talk.
Don't interrupt.
Don't make a move.
Don't be aggressive.
Don't ask questions.
Don't push an agenda.
Don't be possessive.
Don't force anyone.
Don't say "let's FUCK".
Don't say "I LOVE you".

Stay calm.
Stay silent.
Show restraint.
Listen.

Because less is more.

"The Don"
17.03.2021

Things That Money Can't Buy

(Cose che i Soldi non Possono Comprare)

I like things that money can't buy.
Call me crazy.
Call me insane.
Call me weird.
Call me anti-social.
Call me anti- Capitalist.
Call me Socialist.
Call me a *"non-conformist"*.
Call me a *"Radical"*.
I like things that money can't buy.

Things such as:
Integrity.
Principles.
Friendship.
Kindness.
Compassion.
Caring.
Sharing.
Equality.
Humanity
Sensuality.
Passion.
Connection.
Empathy.
LO♥E.
I like things that money can't buy.

All those things that money CAN'T buy.
Like YOU!
It can't buy YOU!
I like things that money can't buy.

"Money is not everything. Who cares about expensive things? It seems like everyone but me. I don't need a man to flash cash in my face. I don't need gifts, to feel good about myself. All I need is a hug in the morning, and a tender kiss goodnight. Sweet dreams."

(Inspired by a conversation with my friend Kim)

"The Don"
17.03.2021

The No Coffee Blues
(Il No Caffè Blues)

I wake up in the morning.
With my head as heavy as lead.
I can't stop myself from yawning.
As I stumble outta of bed.
I've got the no coffee blues, baby.

Yes, that's what I said.
I've got the no coffee blues, baby.

I got wake up my head.
I've got the no coffee blues, baby.

Otherwise, baby, I'm gonna be dead.
I've got the no coffee blues, baby.
Did you hear what I said?
I've got the no coffee blues, baby.

Already I'm beginning to turn red.
I've got the coffee blues, baby.
Otherwise, I'm gonna hide in the shed.
I've got the no coffee blues, baby.

If I don't get some coffee soon, baby.
You know I'm gonna end up dead.
I've got the no coffee blues, baby.

Yes, I do.
I've got the no coffee blues, baby.
Yes, that's true.
I've got the no coffee blues, baby.

Do hear me crying.
I've got the no coffee blues, baby.
No, I ain't lying.
I've got the no coffee blues, baby.

There's nothing else to do.
I've got the no coffee blues, baby.
Yes, yes, yes.
I've got the no coffee blues, baby.

Oh, oh, oh, oh.
I've got the no coffee blues, baby.
Yeah, yeah, yeah, yeah
I've got the coffee blues, baby.

The no coffee blues,
The no coffee blues.
Where's my coffee?
I need my coffee.
Do you hear me?
Anyone out there listening?
Doesn't anybody care about me?
I have the no coffee blues.

And make sure it's the good stuff.
Single origin.
From Brazil.
None of that *"instant"* shit.
That ain't even coffee.
I have the no coffee blues.

"The Don"
19.03.2021

Destiny

(Destino)

What is your destiny?
Do you even believe in it?
We all want to know what it is.
What our future holds.
What our future will be.
What is your destiny?

Will you be rich?
Will you be poor?
Will you be happy?
Will you be loved?
Will you have a family?
Will you be dead?
What is your destiny?

You can go to a fortune teller?
You can read the stars.
You can have your tarot cards read.
You can have your palm read.
You can have your tea leaves read.
You can have your coffee read.
There are many ways to find out....
... your destiny.
What is your destiny?

Some believe religion has the answers.
Some believe in the ancient mystics.
Some believe in Eastern gurus.
Some believe in the ancient runes.
Some believe the Chinese sticks.
Some believe in an altered consciousness.
Some believe in a "conscious" Universe.
What is your destiny?

What do you believe in?

"The Don"
19.03.2021

There Are No Answers
(Non ci sono Risposte)

Don't seek "The Truth".
There is no "Truth".
Don't seek "The Treasure".
There is no "Treasure".
Don't seek " The Mysteries".
There are no "Mysteries".
Don't seek "The Light".
There is no "Light".
Don't seek a "Higher Knowledge".
There is no "Higher Knowledge".
Don't seek a "Higher Power".
There is no "Higher Power".
Don't seek "Spirituality".
There is no "Spirituality".
Don't seek "Higher Levels of Consciousness".
There are no "Higher Levels of Consciousness".
Don't seek "Immortality".
There is no "Immortality".
Don't seek "The Answers".
There are no "Answers".

There just "IS".

"The Don"
20.03.2021

Reality

(Realtà)

Everyone lives in their own world.
It is their world & their world alone.
Everyone has their own world.
Everyone's world is different.
No two worlds are the same.
Their world is their "Reality".
What is your "Reality"?

No world is better or worse.
It is simply yours & yours alone.
Problems arise when we start to equate our "Reality" to the "Truth".
When we start to externalise our world.
When we start to believe that our world is the best.
That our world is better than everybody else's.
That OUR "Reality" is the BEST "Reality".
That OUR "Reality" is the ONLY "Reality".

"Violence" is when we impose our *"World"* onto others.
When we try to deny another person's *"Reality"*.
This act of imposition is *"Violence"*.
This act of imposition can be done in a variety of ways.
The simplest & the most brutal is physical force.
But there are much more subtle forms such as, religious, economic, emotional & psychological.
Realise that your "Reality" is yours & yours alone.

There will be of course, similarities & over peoples' *"Realities"*.
"Reality" is subjective.
"Reality" is not the *"Truth"*.
There are as many *"Realities"* as there are humans living on this planet.
That's a hell of a lot of *"Realities"*.
Do not impose your "Reality" onto others?

"The Don"
20.03.2021

Wants & Needs

(Desideri e Bisogni)

I want YOU but *I don't need YOU.*
I want you to be with me but *I don't need you to be with me.*
I want your intimacy but *I don't need your intimacy.*
I want your friendship but *I don't need your friendship.*
I want to be your friend but *I don't need to be your friend.*
I want to go out with you but *I don't need to go out with you.*
I want to help you but *I don't need to help you.*
I want you to help me but *I don't need you to help me.*
I want you to come over but *I don't need you to come over.*
I want you to stay but *I don't need you to stay.*
I want to hold you but *I don't need to hold you.*
I want you to hold me but *I don't need you to hold me.*
I want to hug you but *I don't need to hug you.*
I want you to hug me but *I don't need you to hug me.*
I want to kiss you but *I don't need to kiss you.*
I want you to kiss me but *I don't need you to kiss me.*
I want to touch you but *I don't need to touch you.*
I want you to touch me but *I don't need you to touch me.*
I want to see you naked but *I don't need to see you naked.*
I want to take you to bed but *I don't need to take you to bed.*
I want to sleep with you but *I don't need to sleep with you.*
I want to FUCK you but *I don't need to FUCK you.*
I want your LOVE but *I don't need your LOVE.*
I want to make LOVE with you but *I don't need to make LOVE with you.*
I want you to LOVE me but *I don't need you to LOVE me.*
I want you in my WORLD but *I don't need you in my WORLD.*

"The Don"
21.03.2021

Everything is Absurdity

(Tutto è Assurdo)

Stop making sense.
Stop trying to figure it out.
Stop looking for answers.
Stop searching for a "meaning".
Stop looking for LO♥E.
Because everything is Absurdity.

Everything is nonsense.
Everything is meaningless.
Everything is fruitless.
Everything is futile.
Everything is a joke.
Everything is Absurdity.

There is chaos everywhere.
There is Death & destruction all around.
There is inhumanity & injustice.
There is pain & suffering.
There is inequality & exploitation.
There is Absurdity everywhere.

Rejoice in the nothing.
Rejoice in the meaninglessness.
Rejoice in the chaos.
Rejoice in the futility.
Rejoice in the horror.
Rejoice in the Absurdity.

Absurdity is everywhere.
There is nothing you can do about it.
It's always been this way.
You born in Absurdity & you will die in Absurdity.
Your life is an Absurdity.
Accept your Absurdity.

Absurdity is fun.
Absurdity is happiness.
Absurdity is society.
Absurdity is LO♥E.
Absurdity is LIFE.
Enjoy your Absurdity.

I LO♥E *Absurdity!*

"The Don"
25.03.2021

A Civilised Society

(Una Società Civilizzata)

We are a *"civilised"* society.
Or so they say.
But are we really that *"civilised"*?
By whose definition are we *"civilised"*?
Who has made this grand statement?
Not me, that's for sure!
I wasn't asked,
"Are we a "civilised" society?"

Let's take a closer look at our so called, *"civilised"* society.
There is:
. *hatred,*
. *fear,*
. *mistrust,*
. *discrimination,*
. *exploitation,*
. *injustice*
. *violence,*
. *inequality,*
. *war*
. *poverty,*
. *hunger,*
. *mass genocide*
. *Inhumanity.*

And this is supposed to be a *"civilised"* society?
Is this what a *"civilised"* society is supposed to look?
I would hate to imagine what an *"uncivilised"* society would look like!

This is NOT a *"civilised"* society.
Let's not kid ourselves.
This is a brutal, uncaring & violent society.
Far from a *"civilised"* society!

"The Don"
25.03.2021

Put Yourself in my Shoes
(Mettiti nei miei Scarpe)

Is that ever, possible?
To put yourself in someone else's shoes?
To see things through their eyes?
To feel what they felt?
To truly understand what they were going through?
To truly appreciate their situation?
To have complete empathy with their actions?

Maybe not.
I don't know if it's ever possible.
We seem to be stuck in ourselves.
Unable or unwilling to step outside ourselves.
I think it's fear that inhibits us.
We are threatened by what we might see.
We fear that we may be wrong.
That maybe there was another angle,
... *another side,*
... *another story,*
... *another interpretation,*
... *another point of view,*
... *that we did not consider.*

Only time will tell if this is possible.
As yet nothing.
I am still guilty.
I am still a bastard.
I am still an arsehole.
I am still a "bad" friend?

There is nothing I can do to change her mind.
Nothing I can do to change the situation.
Nothing I can do to make things better.
Nothing I can do to rectify those events.
Nothing I can do to repair our friendship.
Only time will tell if she can put herself in my shoes.

"The Don"
25.03.2021

Everything is a Scam

(Tutto è Una Truffa)

Everything is a sham.
Everything is a fake.
Everything is a take.
Everything is an illusion.
Everything is a delusion.
Everything is a scam.

Have you ever been scammed?
Maybe you are the scammer?
Maybe you are the faker?
Maybe you are fake?
Maybe you are a stalker?
Maybe you are a troll?
Because everything is a scam.
Everything is a scam.

Have you ever been played?
Maybe you are the player?
Maybe you like to deal?
Maybe you like to steal?
Maybe you like to fake it?
Maybe you like to pretend?
Maybe you're not even real?
Maybe you are not who you say you are?
Everything is a scam.

We are all being played.
We are all being taken as fools
We are all being taken for a ride.
We are all being sucked in.
We are all being taken as suckers.
We are all being duped.
We are all being taken as dopes.
We are all being taken as stoopid.
We are all being stoopid.
Everything is a scam.

"The Don"
25.03.2021

We All Judge a Book by its Cover
(Tutti noi Giudichiamo un Libro dalla Copertina)

It's all about looks.
It's all appearances.
It's all about image.
It's all about presentation.
It's all about the package.
It's all about the outside.
It's all about what we look like.
We all judge a book by its cover.

We all do it.
We have no choice.
We are conditioned.
We are brought up this way.
We make decisions based on appearance.
We judge based on looks.
We choose one person over another, using this criteria.
We all judge a book by its cover.

It's all based on what we find appealing.
It's all based on what the eyes like.
This is what *"Tinder"*, *"Hinge"*, *"Bumble"* & all the other "so called" dating websites are based on...
... *looks*,
... *appearance*,
... *image*.
It's a *"meat"* supermarket.
It's not about *"connection"*.
It's not about a deeper *"spiritual"* idea.
There is no *"mystical"* component in all this.
We all judge a book by its cover.

We like a person based on what they look like.
We like a person based on their appearance.
This is the first thing that we notice.
This is the first thing that we see.
How a person looks like.
If they fit into our box of "likes".
"You are my type!"
"You are not my type!"
It's nothing deeper than that.
It's very superficial really.
Let's not make it out to be more than what it is.
We all judge a book by its cover.

When I say you are…
… *beautiful,*
… *handsome,*
… *desirable,*
… *sexy,*
… *sensual,*
… *exotic,*
… *erotic.*
... I'm saying, that *"I like the way you look!"*
"I like your appearance".
We all judge a book by its cover.

"The Don"
26.03.2021

Pussy Power

(Potere della Figa)

Well, you've heard of….
…."horsepower",
…."wind power",
…."wave power",
…."tidal power",
…."solar power".
…."geothermal power",
…."atomic power",
…."nuclear power".
We've all heard of "manpower".
Now it's time for *"Pussy Power"*.

It's all about *"Girl Power"*.
It's all about empowerment.
It's all about reclaiming your place at the table.
It's all about equal rights.
It's all about equality.
It's all about *"Pussy Power"*!

Power to the *"Pussy"*.
The "Cock" has ruled for far too long!
It's caused massive amounts of destruction.
It's left devastation in its wake.
It's time for the "Cock" be dethroned.
It's time for the "Cock" to be brought down.
It's time for the "Cock" to be put to rest.
It's time for the "Pussy" to take control.
It's time for *"Pussy Power"*!

"Pussy Power"!
"Pussy Power"!
"Pussy Power"!
"Pussy Power"!

"Cock Power" is DEAD!
It's *"Pussy Power"* time!

"The Don"

Zen and the Art of Being

(Zen e l'arte di Essere)

Be still.
Be silent.
Be thought-less.
Be mind-less.
Be motionless.
Be peaceful.
Be *"centred"*.
Be *"equilibrated"*.
Be *"balanced"*.
Be *"enlightened"*.
Be *"Cool"*.
Be easy.
Be *"Fluidic"*.
Be mellow.
Be formless.
Be a shadow.
Be invisible.
Be nothing.
Be free.
Be.
Be *Zen*.
Be Zen and the Art of Being.

"The Don"
27.03.2021

Gatinha (Brazilian Babe)

(Gatinha - Ragazza Brasiliana)

What is it about Brazilian girls?
What do they have?
What makes them so desirable?
What makes them so sensual?
What makes them so exotic?
What makes them so sexy?
What makes them so sexual?
What makes them so erotic?

Maybe it's the way they talk?
Brazilians speak Portuguese NOT Spanish.
NEVER say Spanish.
They will bite your head off.
It is very musical.
Maybe it's the music?
They do have music inside their veins…
…Inside their blood.
…Inside their body.
Maybe it's because they can dance?
Man, can they dance!!!

And when they dance…
When they move their bodies...
I become breathless…
I gasp for air....
I can't breathe...
I faint!
Maybe it's their attitude?
They are very self-confident.
They KNOW that they are sexy!
Maybe it's because they invented *"The Brazilian"*.
Maybe, it's just an undefinable, intangible quality.
That thing that makes them uniquely *"Brazilian Babes"*.
That makes them a *"Gatinha"*!

"Gatinhas" have...
... attitude,
... spunk,
... hootspa,
... fire,
... personality,
... balls.
Don't mess around with a *"Gatinha"*.
If you aren't prepared!
If you're weak.
If you're timid.
If you're not ready for a fight.
If you're not prepared for the battle.
If you don't have *"coglioni"*, Italian for *"balls"*.
Otherwise, the *"Gatinha"* will eat you for breakfast!

Oh, how I LO♥E a *"Brazilian Babe"*.
Oh, how I LO♥E a *"Gatinha"*.

(Dedicated to Amanda Rodrigues daSilva a "real life" Gatinha)
("Lotus Flower Café", Glebe)

"The Don"
29.03.2021

I am a Phlebotomist

(Sono un Flebotomo)

I am a vampire.
I like to suck blood.
I want to suck YOUR blood.

Don't worry, you have enough.
I won't take too much.
Just enough to make me HIGH.
I am a professional.
I do this for a living.
I am a Phlebotomist.

I LO♥E blood!
I LO♥E the colour of blood!
I LO♥E the look of blood.
I LO♥E the sight of blood.
I LO♥E the smell of blood.
I LO♥E the taste of blood
I LO♥E the drinking of blood.
I LO♥E to drink your blood.

Don't worry, it's completely safe.
I know what I'm doing.
I am a professional.
I do this for a living.
I am a Phlebotomist.

It won't hurt at all.
Well maybe, just a little bit.
Just a tingle.
Just a little prick.
You can trust me.
I'll be gentle.
This is not my first time.
I'm not a virgin.
I've done it many times before.

Don't worry, it's completely safe.
I know what I'm doing.
I am a professional.
I do this for a living.
I am a Phlebotomist.

I want suck your blood!
Let me suck your blood!
I love sucking your blood!
Hmmm.......
..... yummy, yummy!
I love blood.
Give me blood!
Blood!
Blood!
I want blood.
Your blood.
I want to take your blood.
I am a Phlebotomist.

(Inspired by Amanda a "real life" Phlebotomist)

"Give blood.
But you may find that blood is not enough.
Give blood.
And there are some who'll say it's not enough.
Give blood.
But don't expect to ever see reward.
Give blood.
You can give it all but still asked for more.

So, give love and keep blood between brothers.
Give love and keep blood between brothers.
Give love and keep blood between brothers.
Give love and keep blood between brothers."

Written by Pete Townshend

"The Don"
29.03.2021

China Girl

(ragazza Cina)

I met here at Sappho Bar.
She sat down near me.
She was with a friend.
I was listening to a guy play guitar & sing.
He was Irish.
He was good.
It was a Saturday night.
It was a full moon.
That's when I met my *China Girl*.

I don't remember how we got to talking.
But I felt a connection straight away.
She said that she had read poetry here before.
I told her I also wrote poetry.
I gave her one of my books.
I read her a few of my latest poems.
She said she hadn't written for a while.
I asked her *"why not?"*
I think she said lack of inspiration or something similar.
I told her she must write.
"Whatever comes into your head".
"Don't censor yourself."
"Don't edit anything".
I told my *China Girl*.

I asked her for a cigarette.
I told her I smoked tobacco but had forgotten it at home.
She said sure.
We hit it off immediately.
I asked them both back to my place for drinks.
"It's just around the corner".
"I've got some dope too".
I asked them if they smoked.
They said they'd like to.
They agreed to come.
Her friend, myself & my *China Girl*.

They both drank wine.
I drank my usual G& T.
We listened to music.
We smoked some joints.
I asked her for a dance.
We started to dance.
We got close.

She was very sensual.
She was grooving.
I held her.
We sat down.
I kissed her on the neck.
I stroked her back.
I was falling for my *China Girl*.

I took off her sandals.
I massage feet.
She was enjoying it.
Her friend was feeling uncomfortable.
He said so.
I stopped.
He said that China Girl was having her periods.
I said, *"how do you know that?"*.
China Girl said that they tell each other everything.
I asked China Girl to dance once again.
She was enjoying the music.
We were both into it.
Her friend moved seats.
He now sat between us.
I was now facing my *China Girl*.

I asked them straight out.
"What was the situation between them?"
"I didn't want to cause any problems".
"I just wanted to clarify the situation".
They replied that they were just good friends.
He said that they had slept together.
I said to him, *"you don't mind if I ask her to stay?"*
He replied that it was up to her.
I realised then that he was her *"protector"*.
Her *"Guardian Angel"*.
I went over & kissed her on the lips.
She did not object.
She did not refuse.
I kissed my *China Girl*.

China Girl did not stay the night.
I messaged the next day.
I asked her if see would like to see me again.
She replied, *"It was a fun night. I'll see you around"*.
I said *"cool"*.
That was my night with my *China Girl*.
Will I ever see her again?
Who knows what the future will bring?
For me & my *China Girl*.
That was my night with my *China Girl*.

"The Don"
30.03.2021

Better to BURN than to RUST
(Meglio BRUCIARE che ARRUGGERE)

Better to run than to walk.
Better to smile than to frown.
Better to drink than to abstain.
Better to be awake than to sleep.
Better to be "weird" than to be "normal".
Better to be funny than to be serious.
Better to be kind than to be unkind.
Better to care than not to care.
Better to RESPECT than to DISRESPECT.
Better to be compassionate than uncompassionate.
Better to be poor than to be rich.
Better to be HAPPY than UNHAPPY.
Better to get HIGH than to be LOW.
Better not to think than to think.
Better to be political than apolitical.
Better to stay young than to grow old.
Better to be less than more.
Better be principled than unprincipled.
Better to be moral than immoral.
Better to be ethical than unethical.
Better to good than bad.
Better to be disobedient than obedient.
Better to be an anarchist than to be compliant.
Better to give than to receive.
Better to be Socialist than Capitalist.
Better to be revolutionary than reactionary.
Better to be Spiritual than Religious.
Better to fuck than to be celibate.
Better to be dis-attached than attached.
Better to be open-minded than closed-minded.
Better to see than to be blind.
Better to be silent than the speak.
Better to listen than to talk.
Better to Live than to Die.
Better to LO♥E than to HATE.
Better to be HUMANE than INHUMANE.
Better to BURN than to RUST.

"The Don"
02.04.2021

GOD is DEAD

(Dio è Morto)

GOD is DEAD.
That's for sure.
But who killed him?
Was it me?
Maybe it was.
I'm not really sure.
Am I to blame for his demise?
Will I take the fall?
Will I be crucified?
But there is no doubt about it.
GOD is DEAD.

Shall we mourn his death?
Shall we cry because he's no longer with us?
Shall we miss him because he's gone?
Shall we be able to cope without him?
Shall we be lonely without his companionship?
Shall we be lost without him to guide us?
Shall we be able to see without his light?
Shall we be able to LIVE?
Since....
GOD is DEAD.

Did we ever need him in the first place?
Did he even exist?
Was he just a myth to begin with?
Were we all duped into believing a lie?
Were we all conned by religion?
Were we all deceived?
Were we all tricked into believing a fairy tale?
That there was NO God to begin with?
That is why I say....
"GOD is DEAD".

Let's put him to rest.
Let's bury him for good.
Let's forget about him.
Let's move on without him.
Let's celebrate a new beginning.
Let's rejoice in a new world.
A world in which we stand on our own two feet.
Without the need of a GOD.
Is it possible?
I think it is.
Because...
GOD is DEAD.

"The Don"
03.04.2021

I Make Lo♥e, NOT Fuck

(Faccio l'Amore, NON Scopare)

I make Lo♥e, NOT fuck.
A big difference.
Your pleasure, is my pleasure.
Your ecstasy, is my ecstasy.
Your HIGH, is my HIGH.
Your orgasm, is my orgasm.
I make Lo♥e, NOT fuck.

Fucking is purely physical.
It's very selfish.
It's all about self-pleasure.
It's all about gratuitous self-satisfaction.
It's all about the individual.
It's all about individual satisfaction
It's all about me.
I make Lo♥e, NOT fuck.

Making Lo♥e, on the other hand……
It's all about the other person.
It's not selfish.
It's not about self-pleasure.
It's not about gratuitous self-satisfaction.
It's not about the individual.
It's not about individual satisfaction
It's not about me.
I make Lo♥e, NOT fuck.

Making Lo♥e is about the other person.
It's about pleasuring the other person first.
It's about satisfying the other person's needs.
It's about satisfying the other person's wants.
It's about fulfilling the other person.
It's about putting the other person first.
It's about putting the other person before my pleasure.
It's getting my pleasure from feeling & experiencing the other person's pleasure.
I make Lo♥e, NOT fuck.

Do you?

"The Don"
05.04.2021

Less is More #2

(Meno è Meglio #2)

We all want control.
We all want power.
We all want to possess.
We all want to own.
We all want friendship.
We all want to affection.
We all want sex.
We all want to FUCK.
We all want Lo❤e.
But less is more.

We all plan.
We all theorise.
We all strategize.
We all lie.
We all fake.
We all elaborate.
We all boast.
We all manipulate.
But less is more.

We need to just BE.
We need the Universe to act through us.
We need to let events unfold as they should.
We need to let situations flow.
We need to let the Future happen.
We need to let Go.
We need to stop stressing.
We need to stop trying to control events.
We need to stop trying to control the Future.
We need just "Let it Be!"
Because less is more.

Don't say too much.
Don't boast.
Don't overplay your cards.
Don't be the "centre of attention".
Don't exaggerate.
Don't manipulate.
Don't overstep the mark.
Don't go beyond the boundaries.
Because less is more.

"The Don"
07.04.2021

Life is a Funny Thing
(La Vita è Una Cosa Divertente)

Life is a funny thing.
Full of twists & turns.
Full of unexpected situations.
Full of "Dejá Vu" experiences.
Full of surprises.
Full of coincidences.
Full of bizarre events.
Full of interesting adventures.
Full of amazing moments.
Full of unimaginable evenings.
Full of unpredictable occurrences.
Full of predictable events.
Full of repetition.
Full of obstacles & hurdles.
Full of potholes & barriers.
Full of traps & dangers.
Full of anguish & disappointments.
Full of pain & suffering.
Full of backwards & forwards.
Full of regression & progression.
Full of hope & achievements.
Full of "WOW" moments.
Full of beauty.
Full of sadness.
Full of loss.
Full of tears.
Full of laughter.
Full of friendship.
Full of dreams.
Full of nightmares.
Full of hatred.
Full of Lo♥e.
Life is a funny thing.
So don't take it too seriously.

"The Don"
09.04.2021

I Don't Give a FUCK

(Non me ne Frega un CAZZO)

I don't care.
I don't scare.
So don't fuck with me.
Cause I'm a bitch.
My name is Erin
My name is Sarah.
My name is Courtney.
Don't mess around with me.
Because I don't give a fuck.

I will punch you.
I will stick my stilettos in your face.
I will have your balls.
I don't care about you.
I can do whatever the FUCK I want.
When I want.
With whom I want.
Because I don't give a fuck.

I don't need you.
I don't need you to tell me what to do.
I don't need you to tell me where to go.
I don't need you at all.
I can PLEASURE myself.
I am my own boss.
Because I don't give a fuck.

I don't give a FUCK about you!
I don't need you.
I am an independent thinker.
I am a free spirit.
I am a free soul.
I am a WILD child.
I have a WILD HE♥RT.
Because I don't give a fuck.

So, leave me the FUCK alone.
'cause I don't give a fuck!

(Inspired by Erin whom I meet @ Ziggy's Wine Bar, Glebe)

"The Don"
11.04.2021

Anal Delights

(Delizie Anali)

Do you like anal?
Can I put it up your arse?
It's all the rage.
Everyone is doing it.
Why not you?
Get some *"Anal Delights"* into you!

Let me enter.
Don't be shy.
Don't hesitate.
I'll be gentle.
It's ok.
You'll enjoy it.
Trust me.
There's NOTHING better than *"Anal Delights"*.

Can I do it you babe?
I'll put my finger in first.
Then I might use a "strap-on".
Let me enter.
Don't be shy.
Don't hesitate.
I'll be gentle.
It's ok.
You'll enjoy it.
Trust me.
There's NOTHING better than *"Anal Delights"*.

Oh NO babe!
How come, babe?
It's ok for you to stick your cock up my arse!
But it's NOT ok for me to stick one up yours!
That's a bit rich!
That's a bit unfair!
Oh, come on, let me enter.
Don't be shy.
Don't hesitate.
I'll be gentle.
It's ok.
You'll enjoy it.
Trust me.
There's NOTHING better than *"Anal Delights"*.

"The Don"
12.04.2021

Tattoo Me

I Lo♥e tattoos.
I want them all over my body.
I am the tattooed woman.
I am the tattooed man.
Come on over.
Have a look at me.
Look very carefully.
Each tattoo tells a story.
I am a story book.
My tattoos are its pages.

Read me.
Take your time.
I'm not going anywhere.
I have nowhere that I have to be.
I am all yours.
Immerse yourself in my pages.
Let yourself be transported to another time & place.

And when you're finished with me…
…be on your way.
Don't look back.
I won't be there.
I will be gone.
To my next reader of my tattoos.
I am not for everyone or just anyone.
I am only for those that a *"Special"*.
Those that don't need their eyes to see.
Those that see without using their eyes.
Those that can *"see"* with their *"3rd Eye"*.
You will know if you are one.
Because only you can *"see"* me.
I will only stop for you.
So that I can be yours for the night.

Come on over.
Have a look at me.
Look very carefully.
Each tattoo tells a story.
I am a story book.
My tattoos are its pages.

Read me.
Take your time.
I'm not going anywhere.
I have nowhere that I have to be.
I am all yours.
Immerse yourself in my pages.
Let yourself be transported to another time & place.

For I am the tattooed woman.
I am the tattooed man.
I have tattoos all over my body.
I am completely covered.
Even my face.
I am the *"Illustrated Woman"*.
I am the *"Illustrated Man"*.
I wear my life on my body.
Read me.
Tattoo me.

"The Don"
12.04.2021

I Saved You Once Again
(Ti ho Salvato Ancora unaltra volta)

Was it, *"being at the right place, being at the right time?"*
Or was it, *" being at the wrong place, being at the wrong time?"*
Who knows?
But there I was.
It happened again.
I couldn't believe it.
Was this really happening again.
Was I completely delusional?
This couldn't be real?
No FUCKING way!
But it was *"real"* enough.
The Universe had conspired to make it so.
There was nothing I could do about it.
It was completely out of my hands.
"Higher" powers were at work here.
All I could do was play out my part.
The script had already been written.
I just had to play out my role.
Which I did.
And she played out hers.

We both knew our parts very well.
We had played them before.
We knew every line by heart.
We knew every move, gesture & emotion.
She played her part perfectly.
Of course, so did I.
We are both, true professionals.
We take our craft seriously.
We won't let the scene down.
We will provide exactly what it requires.
We work so easily together.
Almost like lovers.
But we are not lovers.
We are just actors playing our parts.
But others watching would swear that we were lovers.
But this is why we were chosen for these parts.
We are naturals together.
We make it *"look"* real.
We work well together.
No one believes that we are not lovers in *"real"* life.

It is true that I once had a *"thing"* for her.
But that was a long time ago.
When I was young & innocent.
Still new in my chosen profession.
When I easily confused personal & professional.
She never made that sort of mistake.
She had been doing this for a very long time.
I heard somewhere that she had started when she was just sixteen.
Ah, sweet sixteen.
I was new to this.
I had only started a year or so ago.
I was still *"wet behind the ears"*.
I *"new born baby"*.
A *"babe in arms"*.
I was still naive.
Easily consumed by the situation.
Not controlling my emotions.
Like a truly *"great"* actor should.
But that was a long time ago.
And a lot of *"water has passed under the bridge"* since then.
I am a better actor now.

So, there I was playing out my part.
There was no confusion this time.
I knew what I had to do.
I played my part as written in the script.
I played my role as required.
The ending was a crescendo.
As expected!
As it should be!
Like the ending in *"Casablanca"*.
It is memorable.
Everyone knew the words off by heart.
They have seen this scene a hundred times before.
That tear-jerker...
... where the girl is saved once again.

This was my role.
This was what I did.
I saved you once again.

"The Don"
12.04.2021

Closure

(Chiusura)

The epilogue has finished.
The story has been told.
The ending has been reached.
The curtain has come down.
The song has been sung.
The *"Closure"* has been achieved.

All the loose ends have been tied.
The narrative has concluded.
Everyone lives *"happily ever after"*.
The book has been closed.
The doors have been shut.
The bridge has been withdrawn.
The *"Closure"* has been reached.

Last drinks have been served.
The bar is now closed.
The wounds have all healed.
Reconciliation has been successful.
Everyone walks away happy.
A satisfactory outcome is the verdict.
A happy ending is left.
The *"Closure"* is complete.

(Inspired by my best bro, Miguel)

"The Don"
13.04.2021

Wanker

(Segaiolo)

Are you a "Wanker"?
Do you try to pull the wool over peoples' eyes?
You're a WANKER!
Do talk about your exploits?
You're a WANKER!
Do rave about how good you are?
You're a WANKER!
Do you boast with the guys?
You're a WANKER!
Do you fake it with the girls?
You're a WANKER!
Are you into IMAGE?
You're a WANKER!
Are you "self-obsessed'?
You're a WANKER!
Are you the star of your own war movie?
You're a WANKER!
Are you an arrogant, wannabe guitarist (that delusionally thinks that they are better than Jimi Hendrix)?
You're a WANKER!

Yes!
Hey mate, you're a "Wanker".

Do you wear a ponytail?
You're a WANKER!
Do you wear a suspender belt to hold your pants up (probably because you don't know how to use a belt)?
You're a WANKER!
Do you have a sculptured beard?
You're a WANKER!
Do you have sculptured hair?
You're a WANKER!
Do you drive a lairy car?
You're a WANKER!
Do you drive with loud music blaring out of your speakers?
You're a WANKER!
Do you have a load, noisy, racing car with dual exhausts?
You're a WANKER!
Do you drive a SUV?
You're a WANKER!
Do drive a UTE (but aren't a tradie)?
You're a WANKER!
Do you show off your hairy, fat bum crack when you bend over (not a good look)?
You're a WANKER!
Do you wear white cotton loose baggy clothes?
You're a WANKER!
Are you a "self-awareness" guru?
You're a WANKER!

"Nothing personal!"

"The Don"
14.04.2021

Whatever Happens in "the Moment", Stays in "the Moment"
(Qualunque Cosa Accada nel Momento, Rimane nel Momento)

Laugh in "the Moment".
Fuck in "the Moment".
Lo❤e in "the Moment".
Indulge in "the Moment".
Exist in "the Moment".
Die in "the Moment".
Be in "the Moment".
Live in "the Moment".

Feel "the Moment".
Breathe "the Moment".
Smell "the Moment".
See "the Moment".
Hear "the Moment".
Taste "the Moment".
Experience "the Moment".
Be "the Moment".

Don't fear in "the Moment".
Don't stress in "the Moment".
Don't fret in "the Moment".
Don't miss "the Moment".
Don't hesitate in "the Moment".
Don't waste "the Moment".

All that exists is "the Moment".
For whatever happens in "the Moment", stays in "the Moment".

"The Don"
15.04.2021

Nobody Wants to FUCK a 62 Year Old Man

(Nessuno Vuole Scopare un Uomo di 62 Anni)

Am I finished?
Is it all over for me?
Have I run my last race?
Have I been put out to pasture?
Is this it?
No more girls.
Nobody wants to FUCK a 62 Year old man.

I'm too old.
I'm over the hill.
I'm a *"dirty old man"*.
I'm all washed up.
I'm finished.
This is the end.
Nobody wants to FUCK a 62 Year old man.

How old are you really?
62 years young.
Wow!
You're older than my dad.
Do you like younger woman.
I like all woman.
No matter their age.
I do like older men.
But you might be a little bit "too" old.
Nobody wants to FUCK a 62 Year old man.

Do you have any children?
Yes, a daughter.
How old is she?
29 years young.
Wow!
That's almost my age.
How do you feel about that?
I'm ok about!
Age is not a problem for me.
Is it a problem for you?
Maybe.
Nobody wants to FUCK a 62 Year old man.

Why don't you date woman your own age?
"I find old people generally, very boring.
Either they are preparing to die...
...or they are DEAD already!"
They have nothing to offer me.
They have no vitality....
....no energy....
....no imagination...
....no creativity.
Young people inspire me.
They energise me.
They have LIFE!
But nobody wants to FUCK a 62 Year old man.

Would you like to give me your phone number?
No, I don't think so.
No probs.
Good night.
I walk out onto the footpath.
Another night over.
Another night alone.
Another night in an empty bed.
Nobody wants to FUCK a 62 Year old man.

"The Don"
16.04.2021

A New Day

(Un Nuovo Giornata)

A new beginning.
A new way.
A new say.
A new path.
A new adventure.
A new door.
A new start.
A new chance.
A new *"Reality"*.
A new LIFE.
A new BEING
I'm so happy....
... it's *a new day*.

I'm still alive.
I'm still cognizant.
I'm still functional.
I'm still walking.
I'm still talking.
I'm still laughing.
I'm still HERE....
... wherever *"HERE"* is!
I'm so happy....
... it's *a new day*.

So....
"Carpiem Diem"
"Seize the Day".
Take it by the scruff of the neck....
...& make it yours.
Bend it to your will.
Live life to the full.
Don't waste a moment.
Don't waste a day.
Be *CREATIVE!*
So be happy....
... it's *a new day*.

"The Don"
17.04.2021

Invisible

(Invisibile)

I wear a cloak of invisibility.
No one can see me.
I can see myself.
But nobody else can.
I walk around totally unnoticed.
I sit totally unseen.
I am INVISIBLE.

I can do whatever I want.
I can go wherever I like.
Nobody ever notices me.
I am a phantom.
I am the *"Invisible Man"*.
I am INVISIBLE.

Whenever I speak no one listens.....
....no one hears.
That's why I am VERY loud.
I have to make myself heard.
I have to bring attention to myself.
I have to make myself *"visible"*.
Because I am INVISIBLE.

I do not exist.
I am no one.
I am nobody.
I am a ghost.
I am a *"non-entity"*.
I am INVISIBLE.

"The Don"
18.04.2021

Travelling Light

(Viaggiare Leggeri)

Travel light.
Travel easy.
Travel well.
Travel happy.
Travel joyfully.
Travel musically.
Travel dancing.
Travel SILENTLY.
Travel forwards....
.....(In fact that's the only direction there is!
If you think you're travelling backwards, you're STILL travelling forward!
WTF!
How does that work?
Because, it's ALL in your MIND!)
Travel bright.
Travel TRUE.
Travelling Light.

Travel with a friend &/or many friends *(if possible)*.
Travel with a smile on your face.
Travel with an unfurrowed brow.
Travel with SILENCE.
Travel with the *"LIGHT"*.
Travel with the *"FORCE"*.
Travel with Lo❤e.
Whatever you do....
..... DON'T travel BLUE!
Then......
.....You're *Travelling Light.*

"The Don"
19.04.2021

Every Moment has a Song
(Life is a Musical)

(Ogni momento ha una canzone (La Vita è un Musicale)

Let's live life like we are in a musical.
Like a *"Baz Lurhmann"* film.
Like *"Strictly Ballroom"* or *"Moulin Rouge"*.
Wouldn't it be FANTASTIC!
To break out into a song at every opportunity.
It would make *"Reality"* so much more fun.
In fact, it won't be *"Reality"* anymore.
It would be a *"Musical Reality"*.
For *every moment has a song.*

I Lo♥e scene could have the songs;
"You're as Cold as Ice" or *"Love Hurts"*.
If it was a scene of unrequited love.
Or Love gone bad.
For *every moment has a song.*

All the classics could be used:
"Bad to the Bone",
"Baby Did a Bad, Bad Thing",
"Wicked Game",
"Highway to Hell",
"Back in Black",
"Animal",
"Mistreated",
"Sympathy for the Devil",
"Gimme Shelter",
"Come as You Are",
"Roadhouse Blues",
"Wild Thing",
"Born to be Wild".
For *every moment has a song.*

What a life this would be.
The greatest soundtrack ever.
You would be literally, dancing in the streets.
Cue song "Dancing in the Streets".
See how simple it would be.
Pick you own song.
It's your story.
It's your life.
It's your musical.
For *every moment has a song.*

Every life tells a story.
Every life is a song.
Every life is a musical waiting to be filmed.
Your life is a song.
Your life is a musical.
Your life is a living musical.
Sing, dance, jive, rap!
It's your musical life.
Every song has a moment.
And *every moment has a song.*

Just like all those great musicals from yesteryear.
Like "Oklahoma", "Fiddler on the Roof", "Paint Your Wagon", "Saturday Night Fever, "The Sound of Music", "7 Wives for 7 Brothers" & so on
Life made into a musical.
True life stories embroidered & interwoven into a musical.
Love, sadness, happiness & death turned into songs.
The way life should be.
Life is a Musical.
Every Moment has a Song.

Sing it out loud.
Your life is a song.
Your life is a musical.
Life is a Musical.
Every Moment has a Song.

"The Don"
21.04.2021

I am a Cock

(Sono un Coglione)

I feel with my cock.
I see with my cock.
I taste with my cock.
I hear with my cock
I think with my cock.
I am controlled by my cock.
I am a *"dickhead"*.
I am a cock.

I feel like a cock.
I see like a cock.
I feel like a cock.
I think like a cock.
I do whatever my cock wants.
I am a *"cock head"*.
I am a cock.

My cock is my master.
My cock is my God.
My cock is my mind.
My cock tells me what to do.
I am a servant of my cock.
I am a slave to my cock.
I am a cock.

I am ruled by my cock.
My cock is my brain.
My cock is my mind.
I am a puppet to my cock.
I do my cocks bidding.
I carry out my cock's wishes.
I make Lo♥e with my cock.
I am a cock.

I am a man after all!
What else do you expect?
I am a cock.

"The Don"
22.04.2021

Worship the Pussy
(Adorate la Fica)

Pray to the Pussy.
Kneel to the Pussy.
Idolise the Pussy.
Pay homage to the Pussy.
Light candles to the Pussy.
Burn incense to the Pussy.
Make offerings to the Pussy.
Build a shrine to the Pussy.
Sacrifice yourself to the Pussy.
Devote yourself to the Pussy.
Write poems to the Pussy.
Write songs to the Pussy.
Sing to the Pussy.
Dance to the Pussy.
Be a friend to the Pussy.
Pay your respects to the Pussy.
Show you gratitude to the Pussy.
Worship the Pussy.

Lay down with the Pussy.
Work with the Pussy.
Eat with the Pussy.
Sleep with the Pussy.
Make LO♥E with the Pussy.
Become ONE with the Pussy.
Feed the Pussy.
Lick the Pussy.
Eat from the Pussy.
Drink from the Pussy.
Internalize the Pussy.
Honour the Pussy.
Worship the Pussy.

"The Don"
23.04.2021

He Did Not Look Happy

(Non Sembrava Contento)

He looked decidedly miserable.
He looked *VERY* miserable.
He looked glum.
How looked dishevelled.
He looked *"dazzled"*.
The man with no bum, *"flat pack"*.
He did not look happy.

Maybe he had a *"falling out"*.
It happens every couple of months.
He can only put up with her for so long.
He can only take her for short periods of time.
Before his placid demeanour breaks down.
Before he starts putting demands on her behaviour.
Before he tells her that she's got to stop her erratic ways.
But he did not look happy.

He doesn't really understand her.
He just tolerates her.
She puts out for him.
She is a *"good"* fuck.
She is Brazilian after all.
All Brazilian woman are as *"hot as fuck"*!
We all know that!
He doesn't have to do anything.
She chases him.
He doesn't even know why?
He doesn't even understand her when she speaks.
Her accent is so strong.
He just nods his head politely.
And leaves it at that.
When I saw him walking past me.
...he did not look happy.

Maybe he's always like this.
Maybe he always *does not look happy*!
Because *he did not look happy.*

"The Don"
23.04.2021

Books written by "The Don"

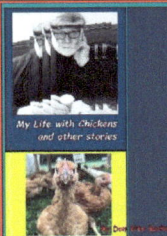
"My Life with Chickens & other stories: I Pity the Poor Immigrant"
Published:
10th September, 2019
Autobiography Book 1:
0 – 12 years old

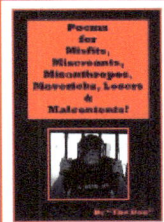
"Poems for Misfits, Miscreants, Misanthropes, Mavericks, Losers & Malcontents!"
Published:
10th June, 2020
Book of Poems 1

"Poems for Troubled Minds & Trouble Hearts"
Published:
10th August, 2020
Book of Poems 2

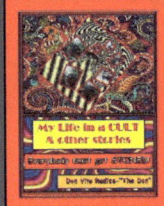
"My Life in a CULT & other stories: Everybody Must Get STONED!"
Published:
10th September, 2020
Autobiography Book 2:
15 – 30 years old

"Poems for Restless Minds & Restless Hearts"
Published:
10th October, 2020
Book of Poems 3

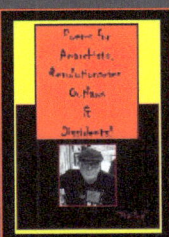
"Poems for Anarchists, Revolutionaries, Outlaws & Dissidents!"
Published:
10th November, 2020
Book of Poems 4

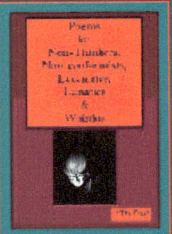
"Poems for Non-Thinkers & Eccentrics"
Published:
10th December, 2020
Book of Poems 5

"The Rantings of a Madman"
Published:
10th January, 2021
Book of Poems 6

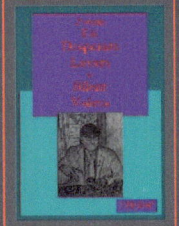
"Poems for Desperate Lovers & Silent Voices"
Published:
10th February, 2021
Book of Poems 7

"Poems for Tormented Minds & Tortured Souls"
Published:
10th March, 2021
Book of Poems 8

All available ONLY online

Books written by "The Don"

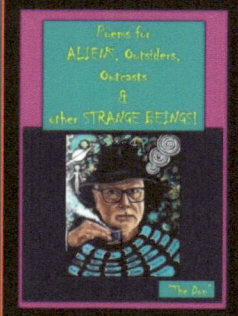

"Poems for ALIENS, Outsiders, Outcasts & other STRANGE BEINGS!"

Published: 10th April, 2021

Book of Poems 9

"Poems for Beings From Another Planet"

Published: 10th May, 2021

Book of Poems 10

"Poems for Mindless Beings & Lost Souls"

Published: 10th June, 2021

Book of Poems 11

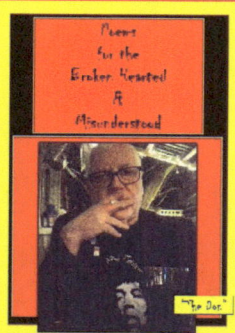

"Poems for the Broken Hearted & Misunderstood"

Published: 10th July, 2021

Book of Poems 12

All available ONLY online

Vito Radice ("The Don"):
Poet/Author/Polemicist/Non-Thinker/Non-Intellectual
To get in touch with "The Don":
Email: donvito7070@gmail.com
Instagram: don_vito_radice
Facebook: Don Vito Radice
Mobile: +61490012461 (Australia)

www.ingramcontent.com/pod-product-compliance
Lightning Source LLC
Chambersburg PA
CBHW041502010526
44107CB00049B/1623